Pray Anyway

Joe McKeever

Parson's Porch Books

www.parsonsporchbooks.com

Pray Anyway

ISBN: Softcover 978-1-951472-14-6

Copyright © 2019 by Joe McKeever

All rights reserved. No part of this book may be reproduced or transmitted in any form or by any means, electronic or mechanical, including photocopying, recording, or by any information storage and retrieval system, without permission in writing from the publisher.

Pray Anyway

Dedication

To my big brother Ronnie.

Rev. Ronald J. McKeever, preacher of God's infallible, inerrant Word for nearly 60 years, pastor of some outstanding churches. Through it all, battling diabetes since you were in your mid-20s. You are a champion and I'm honored to be on the same team as you.

Contents

Introduction 11
   Don't Call Me An Expert On Prayer.

CHAPTER ONE 15
   Have Trouble Praying? No Problem. Just Pray Anyway.

CHAPTER TWO 22
   There's Trouble Ahead. Pray Anyway. 22

CHAPTER THREE 28
   A Prayer for Cleansing

CHAPTER FOUR 34
   The Time I Found I Was Praying All Wrong

CHAPTER FIVE 40
   Five Things We Do Not Know About Prayer

CHAPTER SIX 45
   What God Does When I Pray A Prayer of Repentance

CHAPTER SEVEN 49
   Pray or Else!

CHAPTER EIGHT 53
   The Biggest Problem With Prayer

CHAPTER NINE 62

The Simplest Prayer: "Lord, Help Me!"

CHAPTER NINE 67

Uh, Friend. About Your Poor Prayer

CHAPTER TEN 74

I Prayed For My Preaching--And Got Answers I Did Not Expect.

CHAPTER ELEVEN 81

Why We Pray For Revival and It Does Not Come

CHAPTER TWELVE 87

How To Pray Fresh Prayers

"We do not know how to pray as we should" (Romans 8:26).

No one does. That's no excuse. Pray anyway.

"We see through a glass darkly" (I Corinthians 13:12).

Everyone does. That's no excuse. Pray anyway.

"We who are in this house do groan, longing to be clothed with our dwelling from heaven" (2 Corinthians 5:2).

There's a lot of that going around. That's no excuse. Pray anyway.

Introduction

Don't Call Me an Expert on Prayer.

I'm not sure anyone deserves that honor.

I have two sisters and four brothers, three of whom are with the Lord in Heaven, as are our parents. For the sake of illustration, imagine one of us claiming to be an expert on communicating with Dad and Mom. The others would not let them get by with that. "What's so hard about that?" they would demand. "Mom and Dad are always there, they love us all equally, and they're always pulling for us. Anyone can talk to them!"

They would be offended at one claiming special privilege with our parents.

So, let's not do that. Our Heavenly Father is not remote, not inaccessible, and not hard to talk with.

He is far more willing to hear our prayers than we are to pray. Far more accessible than we are. More willing to bless than we are to receive His gifts.

The problem is us. Not Him.

No one writing a book on prayer should leave the impression that he has found ways into the Father's presence unknown to others, or that he has a magic password granting privileged access into the Throne room.

"We may come boldly to the Throne of grace, that we may obtain mercy and find grace to help in time of need" (Hebrews 5:16). All are welcome, ever since the Lord Jesus became our High Priest.

When Jesus died on Calvary, the veil of the Temple was ripped down the middle, from the top as though the Father took hold of it and opened up free access into His presence from then on. (Matthew 27:51).

So...

We should pray. We may pray. We wisely pray. It's to our benefit, our lasting benefit, to pray!

With this little book, we hope to encourage God's people to pray.

If we can remove some of the impediments to prayer that others have unthinkingly erected, so much the better.

This is not a book you will want to read at one sitting, even though it's short and wouldn't take much time. Each chapter is separate unto itself and addresses a different aspect of prayer.

If you are blessed, I am rewarded.

---Joe McKeever, Ridgeland, Mississippi

PRAY ANYWAY

When you don't know how to pray, pray anyway. Ignorance is no excuse.

When you don't feel like praying, pray anyway. Depression is no excuse.

When dullness sits on you like a vulture, and you can't muster enough energy to check your phone messages, much less to pray, pray anyway. Boredom is no excuse.

When you see no need to pray and no reason to intercede for those about you, recognize this as a sign of impending danger, and pray anyway. Blindness is no excuse.

When you've grown spiritually lazy and feel that you'll never be able to pick up your Bible and read it the way you once did, pray anyway. Laziness is no excuse.

When you don't understand what the big deal is about prayer, and you think it's overrated because it never did you much good, pray anyway. Immaturity is no excuse.

When you're too tired to remember your own name, and you know God will understand if you don't pray, pray anyway. Fatigue is no excuse.

When you're embarrassed to be back before God confessing the same sins and admitting the same failures, come on and pray anyway. Shame is no excuse.

When you've been unfaithful and you know it and you feel that burden of guilt that makes you want to run and hide under the porch, pray anyway. Sin is no excuse.

When the nagging voice of the enemy keeps telling you there is no God and even if there were, He would never have anything to do with a nothing like you, pray anyway. Unbelief is no excuse.

We can bless ourselves immeasurably by rescuing our prayer life from bondage to our emotions and circumstances. There is no time and there are no circumstances in which prayer is not necessary, not helpful, and not the right thing to do. Let us pray.

CHAPTER ONE

Have Trouble Praying?
No Problem.
Just Pray Anyway.

While others spring from the bed each morning eager to spend an hour with the Lord in prayer, do you feel like the only one who has to drag yourself over to a chair and open the Bible and force yourself to think spiritual thoughts?

Welcome to the club.

Others pray smoothly and eloquently and always know what to say; but you are the only one who stumbles along haltingly as though you were just learning to speak or were trying out a foreign tongue.

Sound familiar?

Others are never plagued by doubt and offer up these magnificent sacrifices of praise and intercession that Heaven welcomes, values as jewels, and immediately rewards; you're the only person who fights back the doubts as you pray and wonders whether the whole business is accomplishing anything.

Others see answers to their prayers as a matter of routine; you're the only one who doesn't.

Yeah, right.

It does feel that way sometime.

But it's wrong.

Way wrong. Not so at all.

The fact is those holy people you admire so much for their piety and resent a little for their spiritual maturity fight the same battles you do. They encounter the same temptations, struggle with the same difficulties, and know the same doubts about prayer's effectiveness.

You're not so different.

You're definitely not fighting battles in your spiritual walk others have not faced, or just as likely, struggle with at this very moment.

Two of the Christian faith's heroes, Elisabeth Elliot and C. S. Lewis, have something for us on this subject.

Those who remember Elisabeth Elliot from her lifetime of ministry, or her books and radio programs would agree she is one of the all-time outstanding Christians of any age. She first came to the knowledge of most of us because of the death of her husband, Jim Elliot, martyred by Ecuador's Auca Indians in 1956. Later, after serving as a missionary to those same tribes (alongside other colleagues), she wrote the story that still stands as one of the iconic missionary testimonies, "Through Gates of Splendor."

Inspiring books by this amazing woman will continue blessing God's people until Jesus returns.

You will be interested in knowing Elisabeth Elliot had the same trouble with prayer you and I do.

She said:

"We keep asking the same unanswerable questions and wondering why the explanations are not forthcoming. We doubt God. We are anxious about everything when we have been told quite clearly to be anxious about nothing. Instead of stewing we are supposed to pray and give thanks." (All quotes are from her book, "Trusting God in a Twisted World.")

"When I stumble out of bed in the morning, put on a robe, and go into my study, words do not spring spontaneously to my lips—other than words like, 'Lord, here I am again to talk to you. It's cold. I'm not feeling terribly spiritual….' Who can go on and on like that morning after morning, and who can bear to listen to it day after day?"

She continues, "I need help in order to worship God."

You too, Elisabeth Elliot?

We all do.

Mrs. Elliot found nothing helped her more than reading the Psalms. Sometimes, she wrote, she would open her hymnal and read these offerings of praise to tune her mind to the things of God.

Her spirituality needed jump-starting in the morning.

Just like yours, just like mine.

Elisabeth Elliot asked, "Do you know what to pray for people whom you haven't heard in a long time? I don't." In those cases, she prays prayers found in Scripture, such as the one in Ephesians 3:17-18, "…that you, rooted and founded in love yourselves, may be able to grasp…how wide and long and deep and high is the love of Christ."

And lest we fail to get the point, Elliot adds, "My own devotional life is very far from being Exhibit A of what it should be."

Then there is C. S. Lewis.

Since the death of this English literature professor and brother-in-Christ on the very day President Kennedy was assassinated, Lewis' books on the Christian faith have ministered to every new crop of seeking minds on this planet at a constant pace. His influence shows no sign of waning. His books will never go out of print.

Elisabeth Elliot, along with every other Christian writer, quotes Lewis. She calls him "that wise man who seems to have thought through almost everything…."

Well, surely C. S. Lewis had this prayer business all worked out, right? He wrote so much on everything and his insights and conclusions are infused with such common sense and eureka moments that we read with awe and enjoyment. Certainly, he was one of the elites who do not struggle with doubt but glide effortlessly into prayer in the early morning hours and pray unfalteringly memorable prayers of faith that impress the Heavens and shake the world.

Here are snippets of what Lewis said about his praying.

In a letter to a friend, C. S. Lewis said however badly a good book on prayer is needed, "I shall never try to write it." He added, "For me to offer the world instruction about prayer would be impudence." (All quotes are from "C. S. Lewis, Mere Christian," by Kathryn Ann Lindskoog. She points out that Lewis did indeed write that book on prayer, of course. In fact, he wrote several.)

"He noted wryly that the worse one prays, the longer it takes."

"He found it much easier to pray for others than for himself."

About lists of people to pray for: "Such a long list is burdensome; it makes it a little hard to think about each person while praying."

"He felt it unnecessary to pray for people by name; one may have lost or never known the name of a person who needs one's prayers. He figured God knows their names."

It is possible that our highly respected friend, Mr. Lewis, even had the occasional error in his prayers. Lindskoog writes, "He emphatically believed in praying for the dead!" A couple of verses in the New Testament are given as his reasons (I Corinthians 15:20 and I Peter 3:19-20). While most of us might find those unconvincing, one of the myriad of things we admire about this man is he never demanded that readers agree with him.

I was glad to see that Lewis believed in praying about small, almost inconsequential matters. Lindskoog writes, "Prayers about trivial matters may be good practice, anyway. Lewis felt that high-minded religion tends to be a snare. 'I fancy we may sometimes be deterred from small prayers by a sense of our own dignity rather than of God's.'"

"Near the end of 'Letters to Malcolm: Chiefly on Prayer,' Lewis said that he decided to come clean. He admitted that for most people prayer is a duty, and an irksome duty at that. He observed that we are reluctant to begin and delighted to finish."

I expect most of us knew that, whether we admitted it to ourselves or not. One has to wonder if we have ever admitted it to God. Not that He doesn't know, for He does. Genuine prayer requires a high degree of honesty.

That may be the reason C. S. Lewis often began his prayer time with what he called his "prelude to prayer."

Concerned that his thoughts of himself and of God might be faulty and misleading, Lewis would pray, "May it be the real I who speaks. May it be the real Thou I speak to."

Lindskoog comments, "Lewis didn't want his false idea of himself speaking to a bright blur in his own mind."

In Lewis' "Footnote to All Prayers," he implores the Lord to mercifully translate the false and inferior ideas in his prayers into something that would be acceptable to Himself.

He understands. So does she.

So does He.

"Therefore, let us understand, Father, that even though we come before Thee stumbling and muttering, it's all right. Scripture promises the Spirit will help us in our weakness since we do not know how to pray as we should. Your servant, the Apostle Paul, said that. It helps somewhat to remember that even he had the same struggles as we."

"So do not let the enemy convince us that we alone of all God's children pray poorly. Granted, we are like infants just learning to speak, but we recall how much the tender Father loves those attempts."

"Thank you, Father. You are gracious and loving and it is our honor to be Yours, to enter Thy presence, to offer up our prayers. Amen."

CHAPTER TWO

There's Trouble Ahead.
Pray Anyway.

Looking back over eight decades of life and six of ministry, I think of the potholes I hit and the chasms I plunged into and wish I had been better fortified for such moments.

Or better yet, had missed them altogether.

No one wants to go through heartaches, failures, betrayals, and disappointments. And yet, as Job said to his friends, "Man who is born of woman is short-lived and full of turmoil" (Job 14:1). It seems to go with the territory.

As Grandma told the teenager, "Trouble is not par for the course, honey. It is the course."

The challenge is to be prepared for it.

I wish I had been better prepared for the unexpected, those events and situations and people and temptations that lay in wait for me, just around the corner. Poor, unsuspecting me, I rushed headlong into the day without a clue that a bear trap lay open and set just around the corner.

We've all seen this. An accident on the highway brings traffic in the opposite lanes to a standstill. Emergency workers tend to accident victims, law enforcement officers are everywhere protecting the scene, no motorists are going anywhere. Driving past, in the opposite direction, you see the traffic is backed up for miles. Further down the highway, you come upon drivers who are headed toward that accident scene at 70 and 80 miles per hour. They have no clue what's just ahead, and you have no way of alerting them. You hope they stop in time and do not create new problems.

Life is a lot like that. Trouble lies in wait for you, just ahead. Some disgruntled church member or an outright enemy is loaded for bear and you are about to stumble upon them. Temptation with your name written all over it lurks in the path you have chosen this morning. The company you work for has decided to hand you a pink slip or transfer you to the city of your dreams or the land of your nightmares. A new boss has been hired and he/she has issues with you, even though this morning will be the first time you've met.

You whistle as you stride happily down the sidewalk or into the office. Life is good. You are ready for anything this day hands you.

You think.

Trouble ahead. Be prepared.

This is where prayer does its best work.

Our Lord walked to the gravesite of Lazarus. His friend has lain dead for so long the body was decomposing. The stench was awful. Everyone was watching to see what Jesus would do. As far as they knew, the Lord had never done anything approaching this in magnitude. On other occasions, He had raised a little girl dead one hour and a young man dead for no more than a day. But nothing He had faced comes close to this challenge. He's about to restore to life a man dead for four days.

One of Lazarus' sisters put it in plain language: "Lord, by this time, he stinks" (John 11:39).

The man was dead dead. No question about it.

Jesus did something fascinating and instructive for us. Before calling the man to life, He stopped to pray. We're not surprised by that but look at what He prayed.

"Father, I thank You that You heard me when I prayed." (John 11:41)

Got that? Jesus had already done His praying. He was ready for whatever He encountered that day. He did not have to call time-out for a lengthy prayer meeting. He was prepared.

Prayer had done its work in His life.

Consider the great failure in the life of King David. We could wish he had had the forethought to have prepared for his new life as a retiree by prayer and planning.

"Now, it happened in the spring, at the time when kings go out to battle.... David stayed at Jerusalem. Now, when evening came David arose from his bed and walked around on the roof of the king's house, and from the roof he saw a woman bathing...." (II Samuel 11:1-2)

Nothing was ever the same for David from that moment. Temptation blind-sided him and caught him unaware and he fell headlong into that bottomless pit.

We wonder. What if he had fortified himself with prayer? What if, when his life circumstances began to change ("I'm getting a little old for this warrior bit; it's time to stay at home more"), he had prayed for the Father to strengthen and prepare him for whatever lay ahead? What if he had been watching for temptation and been ready for it? He would have saved himself, his nation, generations of his descendants, and of course the Uriah family incredible grief and misery.

"Pray that you may not enter temptation," said our Lord (Matthew 26:41).

Job said, "I made a covenant with my eyes not to look on a virgin." (Job 31:1) We assume this means he had committed himself in advance not to look lustfully on young women. Had David made such a covenant, he would have done well. Many a fallen servant of God has looked back ruefully and thought the same thing.

"What was I thinking?" (And the still small voice inside answers, "Actually, you weren't.")

"Why wasn't I praying?"

Our Lord gave us the instruction we need for this area and these times of our lives.

"Lead us not into temptation. Deliver us from evil." (Matthew 6:13)

Jesus told His disciples, "When the shepherd puts forth his sheep, he goes before them." (John 10:4)

He goes before the flock, leading us "in the path of righteousness" (Psalm 23:3).

May I offer up a prayer at this point?

"My Lord go before me today. I do not know what tasks and temptations this day holds, what demands I will encounter, what foes may be lying in wait, what opportunities will open before me. Tomorrow is an even greater mystery. I cannot foresee the people I will meet or imagine the situations in which I will find myself.

"Lead me, O Lord.

"I am aware that testing is for my benefit in order to purify and strengthen me. However, I count any day a good one when I was not placed in a critical situation where I could have blown it all and sabotaged the work You are doing in my life.

"Go before me, Jesus, my Shepherd. Make the way safe ahead of me. Lead me in the path of righteousness for Thy name's sake.

"Prepare me for what I will see, be glorified in what I will say and think and do.

"I do not want to stay home in order to avoid all difficulties. In my heart of hearts, I want my life to make a difference in this world. Therefore, I willingly venture into unsafe places for Jesus' sake.

"The enemy awaits, Father. He and his army have laid their improvised-explosive-devices at critical points ahead. Keep me alert.

"Fortify my armor in the places where I will be attacked. Reinforce my faith for the doubts that will arise. Strengthen my mind for the questions, my heart for the stresses, my soul for the demands.

"And when the day is over, may I look back with joy at having sensed Thy presence at key moments, known Thy leadership in crucial decisions, and felt Thy power in moments of weakness.

"Thy will be done in me, O Lord. For Jesus' sake. Forever. Amen."

---ooo000ooo---

The inimitable John R. Rice, in his book Prayer: Asking and Receiving, said, "Prayer is not a touring sedan in which to see all the sights of the city. Prayer is a truck with which we drive to the warehouse, pick up the goods, and return home."

CHAPTER THREE

A Prayer for Cleansing

"Father in Heaven. My Lord and my God. Savior and Redeemer. Friend in my deepest need.

Hear the cry of my heart, feel the pain of my soul, see the need of my life.

Cleanse me of all my sin.

Take away everything in me…

…that does not bow before Thee as Lord.

…that does not have Thy name on it.

…that is resistant to Thy Spirit.

…that is impure and unworthy of Thee.

Remove from me…

…all attitudes and opinions and convictions that do not originate in Thee;

…every desire and motive and plan and ambition in conflict with Thy holy will;

...anything that runs and hides when You enter, that laughs when I believe, that squirms when I pray, that fears when I trust;

...Whatever in me does not give Thee joy, make Thee proud, and serve Thy purpose;

All of this, take away, please...

...everything that holds me back, weights me down, and cheapens my praise,

take away and make me whole.

By the precious blood of Jesus, purge my iniquity.

In the matchless name of Jesus, make me clean.

For the wonderful sake of Jesus, draw me to Thee.

Make me whole and holy and wholesome.

Make me right and upright and righteous.

Give me a heart that wants only to do Thy will, that answers only to Thy call, that serves only to hear Thy 'well done.'

Amen."

Have you ever been so filthy you wanted a bath more than anything else in the world? I have. Growing up on the farm, I can remember those days of baling hay or mucking out hog pens or cattle stalls when you felt like the dirt and smell would stay with you forever.

Have you ever felt that kind of soul-stain that soils and defiles and makes you shrink from reading your Bible or bowing in prayer out of pure shame? I've been there, too.

"We do not know how to pray as we should," said the Apostle Paul (Romans 8:26). If he didn't, it's a safe bet the rest of us don't either. And yet prayer to the Savior is our only lifeline. As Peter said, "To whom (else) shall we go? Thou hast the words of eternal life" (John 6:68)

This prayer is about uprooting every weed in my life, every tare planted by the enemy and maybe one or two I put there myself.

It's about belonging to the Savior and Him alone. Of being rid of all that says no to God's yes. From anything that puts the brakes to the Spirit. That keeps us earthbound when God bids us soar. That dampens our creativity, hinders our freedom, stifles our laughter, smothers our joy, and walls us in from each other.

God wants us free to laugh and sing and serve. To love without fear. To give without regret. To pray without doubt. To worship without limit. To witness to others without a thought to myself. To know how precious I am to Him without undermining it by my low self-esteem. To revel in the promise of glory while enjoying a touch of that glory now.

To be clean is a wonderful thing, but it's only the first thing. "These have washed their robes and made them white in the blood of the Lamb," said a heavenly elder to the Apostle John. "For this reason they are before the throne of God and they serve Him day and night in His temple." (Revelation 7:14-15) To stand and serve in the presence of the Father, that's the main thing.

Being human and lazy and self-indulgent, we prefer to skip the washing. Stand by the door of any public restroom and be horrified at the numbers who parade past the basins and out the doors eager to share their germs with the world.

Just inside the Pediatric ICU, a nurse informed us we would have to wash before being admitted. At a sink operated by foot pedals, we scrubbed, using sanitary brushes saturated with their own soap. "Three minutes, minimum," she said. Three minutes seems like thirty when all you're doing is standing at a sink washing your hands.

"You'd be surprised how resistant germs are," she commented and went on her way.

How resistant sin is. The heart must be washed and purified, the sin uprooted, nailed, cauterized, bleached, and destroyed. Then tomorrow, we will require a fresh session of confession and cleansing once again. Sin is persistent.

No one having light thoughts of sin will never have heavy thoughts of God.

Interestingly, the Bible does not call sin black, as we might expect, but red. "Though your sins be as scarlet," God says, "they shall be as white as snow. Though they be red like crimson, they shall be as wool." (Isaiah 1:18) Ask any mother what a red sock does in the washing machine with a load of whites.

A few years back, as we prepared to enter our new sanctuary, I noticed a red dirt stain on the sidewalk outside the rear entrance. It obviously needed washing down with a pressure scrubber. "We tried that," said a custodian. "But that red dirt was sealed in the concrete by the men who poured it. The only way you can get it out is to remove the sealer, scrub it down, and put a new sealer on the walk."

"Father in Heaven: Today I feel like that sidewalk. Open me up and cleanse me deeply. Then seal me with Thy Spirit. Amen."

---ooo000ooo---

I was flipping channels one night and came upon Pat Boone on a talk show. He was telling about Evangelist Kenneth Copeland. "I knew him before he came to Christ," he said. "And he was rough. When I heard someone mention

Evangelist Kenneth Copeland, I couldn't wait to ask him what God had used to bring him to Jesus. He told me, 'It was nothing in the world except my mother's prayers. My mother stayed in the face of Jesus until He saved her son.'"

CHAPTER FOUR

The Time I Found I Was Praying All Wrong

The other night, a realization threw me out of the bed and drove me to my note pad. I was lying there in the post-midnight hour doing what we preachers do, going over my sermon for later that morning.

The sermon was a beginning of a four-day revival meeting I would be preaching for a congregation in central Louisiana. The church ran 80 to 100 in attendance, mostly farmers and their families. Over dinner the previous evening, the pastor and I prayed for the Lord to give me the messages and do something special in the hearts and lives of his people.

The text for the first revival sermon was the parable of the mustard seed, Matthew 13:31-32. God loves to use small, ordinary things and churches and people and acts and offerings. The mustard seed is a reminder that what God does at first may be unimpressive on the outside, ordinary to the human eye, and not promising. However, being God, He can do amazing things with small beginnings. From nothing if you want to know the truth.

I love to encourage small congregations with the assurance Jonathan gave his armorbearer just before the two of them took on a nest of Philistine warriors.

"It matters little to the Lord whether He saves by the few or the many. (I Samuel 14:6)"

As the prophet Zechariah spoke of the rebuilding of the economy version of the Temple and the coming of a Messiah who would ride on a colt and be pierced for our transgressions, he asked, "Who has despised the day of small things?" (Zech. 4:10)

The answer to that is: "We do." We humans like big things, dramatic results, impressive crowds, celebrity guests. We like glitter, gaudy, loud, impressive.

However, that happens not to be God's way. He loves to use the small and the ordinary.

That's when it hit me that I was praying all wrong about this revival.

I need to be praying for God to do a small thing.

After Hurricane Katrina devastated our part of the world in 2005, we began praying for God to do big things. We printed up cards the size of standard business cards urging people to pray big. On one side, it carried this from John Newton:

Thou art coming to a King.

Large petitions with thee bring.

For His grace and power are such

None can ever ask too much.

On the other side of the card was our prayer request: "Now, we will take a small 'God bless New Orleans' prayer. But we would rather you would pray big. Ask God to do something new, something big, something 'God.'"

And I still believe that.

But that night, God dropped the other shoe.

Sometimes, a small thing from God is enough.

Consider...

...A revival in which one child came to Christ but who grew up to make a lasting difference for God in this world would be the very definition of success.

...A meeting where large numbers respond and are baptized but who cannot be found a month later would be a success only on paper.

Of course, it's not "either/or." At Pentecost, God saved 3,000 souls. And with so many millions in this country and billions on this planet still outside the fold of His saving grace, there is a huge job to do.

But that's why we need to drop back and ask Him to do it His way.

I received an email that troubles me.

A man I do not know had found an article on my blog telling "why we don't want revival." He asked if he could use the piece in his ministry. He went on to explain what he was doing for the Lord. After all, he said, all those Billy Graham crusades over the decades did not make a difference. They were ineffective, he said.

So, God was raising up him to get it right.

I replied that he is surely welcome to use anything of mine he can in his ministry. But I suggested he not be so quick to judge Billy Graham's ministry. There is no way to measure what this country or this world would look like had he not done his worldwide work of evangelistic crusades. I personally know of many who came to Christ through his writings and preaching, and I myself have benefited greatly from his ministry.

So much of what God is doing at a given moment is not visible. And even what we can see may not be all that impressive if I may say so. A hymn, a sermon, an invitation. A testimony. A prayer. An offering. And yet, God is at work there. We must be careful not to despise small things.

Clearly, that brother longed to see large evidence of God at work.

Don't we all.

But when it comes, very likely God's answer will be a small thing here, an ordinary person there, an event that hardly makes the newspapers, a sermon that impresses no one but God.

I keep thinking of a meeting of church leaders following a revival. One man complained. "Preacher, how many people were saved in the meeting last week?"

The pastor said, "We had one child who said he was saved."

"One kid," the man said. "And what did that revival cost us?"

The pastor said, "The honorarium, the travel, motel and meals, plus the publicity, it all came to over $2,000."

"And all for one kid!" he said. "Hardly worth the investment."

With that, one of the men got up, walked to the front of the room, and took out his checkbook. As he began to write, he said, "My friends, that was my boy. And he was worth every penny of it."

A small child with a small lunch. Jesus used it to feed the thousands.

A small baby in a stable in a little town. God used Him to redeem a lost world.

A small sermon today in a small church. God can do anything He pleases.

"Father, forgive me for wanting the big and the dramatic. Forgive me for doubting Your power to

use the infinitesimal to do the infinite. Today, please do a little thing in our midst today. Remind us again and again that a little thing done by an Almighty God is more than enough for all our needs forever. Through Jesus our Lord. Amen."

---ooo000ooo---

In her book *Prodigals and Those Who Love Them*, Ruth Bell Graham tells of the time Monica, mother of the young wayward Augustine, went to her priest for counsel and encouragement. Augustine was breaking her heart over his sinful ways. At the end of the session, the priest told her, "Go! Leave me alone. Live on as you are living. It is not possible that the son of such tears should be lost."

CHAPTER FIVE

Five Things We Do Not Know About Prayer

To be sure, we know a lot about prayer. We know it's of faith—addressing a God whom we cannot see and are unable to prove that He's even there, much less listening to the likes of us—and we know we ought to do more of it and do it better.

But it might be helpful to address some of the things no one knows about prayer.

1. We do not know how to pray as we should.

That's Romans 8:26. "Likewise, the Spirit also helps us in our weaknesses. For we do not know how to pray as we ought, but the Spirit Himself makes intercession for us with groanings which cannot be uttered."

At those times when our prayers seem pitifully small and weak, it helps to remember that even the great apostle—arguably the greatest Christian ever—put into words our own helplessness: "We do not know how to pray as we ought."

This does not stop us from praying. It only assures us that our perfectionism—a killer in most endeavors—does not apply here. Prayer cannot be done perfectly in this life. So, we do what we can, pray as well as we're able, and leave it to the Father to sort it out.

2. We do not know what God is doing in answer to our prayers at any given moment.

Nothing is so much about faith as praying. Not only are we addressing a Deity whom we cannot see or prove, in most cases we never know whether our prayers were even answered or not. And yet, we keep praying. Talk about faith!

You pray for the President of the United States, for a missionary on the other side of the globe, and for your child who heads off to school in the morning. In no case will you be there to see if and how your prayers are answered. The president gets a sudden inspiration and makes a wise decision, the missionary is protected from harm while walking through a dangerous neighborhood, and your child figures something out the teacher has been trying to get across. Your prayers were answered. The only problem is….

You never know it.

If you are careless, you will conclude your prayers are accomplishing nothing and you will go on to other endeavors. As a result, the world grows more dangerous and the people you love more vulnerable because you quit praying.

"In due season we shall reap if we do not quit" (Galatians 6:9).

3. We do not know who else is praying.

Elijah is not the only servant of the Lord who felt like the Lone Ranger (I Kings 19:10). Many times we all get that isolated sense that "I'm the only one left."

It's not true, thank the Lord.

There is no room in the Kingdom of God for the pessimism that drops our chin to our chest, gives up hope, and leaves the playing field before the final gun. We are more than conquerors through Him who loved us (Romans 8:37). We are surrounded by a great cloud of witnesses (Hebrews 12:1), veterans of the same wars we are presently engaged in; they are watching and cheering us on. Furthermore, when we finally turn in our badges and report to our Heavenly assignment, we will be overwhelmed to discover the size of the regiment to which we belonged (see Revelation 5:11 and 7:9, for starters).

Stand strong, Christian. You are in good company.

4. We do not know how things would be if we had not prayed.

In the movie "It's a Wonderful Life," George Bailey was given a gift, the ability to see what the world would have been like had he never been born.

The rest of us are not given that present. We don't even get to see how things would have been had we not been faithful in praying.

We have to take it by faith, at least for the present. The day will come, we are assured, when we will "know as we are known." We see through a glass dimly now, but "then face to face" (I Corinthians 13:12).

We will be so glad we were faithful. Or, so pained that we quit early and left the field.

Jesus asked, "When the Son of Man comes, will He find faith on earth?" (Luke 18:8) Nothing tells the tale on that like our praying.

We pray by faith, disciple of Jesus, or we do not pray at all.

5. We do not know all God did as a result of someone else's prayers.

As a 19-year-old college sophomore, I made a decision that changed everything from that day to this: I joined a wonderful church a mile from the campus. As a result of that one act—and it was about as simple as you can get—I was baptized, later called into the ministry, and then ordained in that church. I met a host of friends who became a great force in my life, including Margaret Ann Henderson, to whom I was married for 52 years before the Lord took her in January 2015.

A thousand things changed as a result of that one act in September of 1959.

I have often wondered: a) Did I pray about the decision before making it? (I may have; I don't recall.) b) Who else was praying? There is no way to know.

Was my mother praying? Another friend or family member? or did the Lord just sovereignly decide to do this without being asked? Or all of the above?

No way to know. But whoever prayed for me, I am forever in their debt.

No one who must have all his/her answers before they begin will ever pray.

No one who depends on his/her feelings as indicators of God's presence and whether He is hearing and answering will ever pray.

No one who cannot live by faith and wait upon the Lord for answers will ever pray.

No one who waits until they can do so perfectly will pray.
No one who uses the prayerlessness of others as an excuse for his own rebellion will pray.

We will pray by faith or not pray at all.

Brethren, let us pray.

And let us pray for friends far and near, almost forgotten or newly acquired, asking God's blessings upon them.
Let us pray for people in the news, knowing we will never meet them in this life, but asking the Father's guidance and provision to be given them.

Let us pray by faith and leave the matter with Him.

CHAPTER SIX

What God Does When I Pray A Prayer of Repentance

It happened again this morning. In the pre-dawn hours I lay awake, unable to sleep. Anxieties were filling the room like ghosts in the night, trying to frighten and alarm me with varying degrees of success, but successfully robbing me of sleep. As always, I lay there sending up little prayers to the Father.

"Forgive me of my sin, Father. Help me. You are my Rock. You are my strength."

Lying there, I thought of all the reasons the Lord has for not hearing me. I'm such a poor Christian. My prayer life is so shallow. I read the Bible in the mornings and rarely give it another thought in the day. He takes care of my financial needs and still I worry. What kind of Christian am I? Why should He forgive me? What if the people I work with knew what a poor Christian I am?

And then this morning, He sent the answer.

I heard the garbage truck outside, running its usual early Saturday morning route. The motor revved as workers compacted the trash. Someone hollered. A metal can hit the pavement. The engine purred as the truck softly moved forward to the next house. The noises were oddly comforting.

And then the Holy Spirit told me why.

The workers are taking away our garbage. The sanitation system has ways of dealing with it, places to dump it, methods for disposing of it. It will be gone; we will never see that trash again. Their system works—our streets are clean, and our homes are free from the continual buildup of accumulated garbage and the unhealthy conditions that would produce. We owe a great debt to workers whom we rarely ever see.

In the same way, God removes the sin we have confessed. It is gone. We will walk outside later this morning and retrieve the garbage cans we set out last night. They will be empty. We will set them back in place inside the fence, ready to receive today's and tomorrow's garbage. That's the process; we believe in it and rarely question it.

Shouldn't we believe God just as strongly and surely? Shouldn't we take as fact that "if we confess our sins, He is faithful and just to forgive our sins and to cleanse us of all unrighteousness." (I John 1:9)

When He takes it away, God removes it totally and deals with it thoroughly. He buries it in the deepest ocean (Micah 7:19). He forgets it (Hebrews 10:17). He nails it to the cross (Colossians 2:14).

The point being, we'll never see that sin again. "As far as the east is from the west, so far has He removed our transgressions from us." (Psalms 103:12)

There's a condition here, though. A "divine however".

The garbagemen—the sanitation workers—only remove what I set out. They do not enter my house and walk through the rooms and comb through the waste baskets gathering up all the trash they can find. That's my job. What I identify as trash and put in the appropriate container and set in place, they will cart away.

My job before the Lord is to identify and name the trash in my life, anything unworthy of Him, everything that interferes with my worship and obedience of Him, all that does not have His name on it, whatever weighs me down and holds me back and hinders faith. "Whatsoever is not of faith is sin," we're told in Romans 14:23.

I make it a point to name anything the Holy Spirit calls to my attention—because He is the One who knows what I need to set on the curb—and then I pray, "Forgive me of all my sin, O Lord."

In confessing it to the Father, I am not removing my sin. I am merely bagging it and setting it on the curb for the Holy Spirit to pick up and deal with.

Because of the great and mysterious process that occurred when our Lord Jesus Christ died on the cross and was resurrected three days later, the system works. His blood atones for my sins. His death paid for my wrongs. He died in my place. He and He alone is the Savior. I am the beneficiary, the heir of His estate, the one blessed by the curse of the cross. Only in Heaven will we learn the full dimension of the blessings that are ours by Calvary.

Human language falters trying to fathom and encapsulate and describe all that is ours as a result of that event on the hill outside Jerusalem some 2,000 years ago.

We know it's not just a matter of saying the right words, of touching all the bases, but in asking the Father for cleansing and forgiveness and for Him to fill me with His Spirit and to use me that day, I ask Him to do this "by the precious blood of Jesus, in the matchless name of Jesus, for the wonderful sake of Jesus."

Now I'm ready to face a new day.

CHAPTER SEVEN

Pray or Else!

Then He spoke a parable to them, that men always ought to pray and not lose heart. (Luke 18:1)

Pray or quit.

Pray or grow discouraged and drop by the wayside.

Pray or weaken and wither away.

If I were the devil, I would do anything within my power to stop God's people from praying.

If I were the devil, I'd be patting myself on the back about now, since it would appear that very few are praying. Well, praying in any sort of meaningful, situation-altering way, anyway.

No one believed in prayer the way the Lord Jesus did.

Perhaps no subject so permeates the four gospels like prayer. Jesus exhibited it, taught it, reminded His disciples of it, and told stories of people who did it well.

Pray or else, disciple of Jesus.

1. Pray or else you will work in the flesh.

"Those who are in the flesh cannot please God" (Romans 8:8).

We have a choice every day of our lives, in every task we undertake: to work in the Spirit or in the flesh. To do it on our own, looking to ourselves for our resources and wisdom, or to turn to Him.

The process of turning to Him is called prayer.

2. Pray or else you will contradict Jesus.

"Without me, you can do nothing," our Lord said in John 15:5.

We are as dependent on our Lord as the branch trying to bear fruit depends on the larger branch (or vine) from which all sustenance comes. To say otherwise, is to call Jesus Christ a liar.

3. Pray or else you are planning to fail.

To the disciples at the foot of the Mount of Transfiguration, our Lord explained why they had been unable to help the little boy who had been brought to him for help. "This kind comes out only by prayer" (Mark 9:29).

Why did our event fail? There may be many reasons, but if you did not lift the matter and yourself to the Lord in prayer, I suggest you put the blame there. "You did not ask," is how James 4:3 puts it.

4. Pray or else you will grow discouraged, lose your way, and we'll have to send out a search and rescue team for you.

The Lord who wants nothing so much as to bless us will not force His will upon us. In one of the most fascinating promises to be found in scripture, Jesus comes right up to the front door with Heaven's blessings and knocks. He says, "If anyone hears my voice and opens the door, I will come into him...." (Revelation 3:20).

It's up to us.

He will allow us to go our way, work in our strength, and to fail–if that's what we choose.

If you are willing and obedient, you shall eat the good of the land; but if you refuse and rebel, you shall be devoured by the sword. For the mouth of the Lord hath spoken. (Isaiah 1:19-20.

5. Pray or else you will find your success hollow, your joy meaningless, your riches empty.

To the rich, myopic, gentleman farmer of Luke 12, God said, "You fool! This night your soul will be required of you; then whose will those things be which you have provided?"

The wasteful, rebellious son of Jesus' parable in Luke 15 found how limited his wealth was, how fickle his friends were, and how fleeting his fun was. Only in the hog pen did he come to his senses and get up and come home to the waiting father.

6. Pray or else you abandon those depending on you.

"Far be it from me that I should sin against the Lord in ceasing to pray for you," said the Prophet Samuel to the nation Israel (I Samuel 12:23).

One night, walking my usual route through the neighborhood, praying and planning and thinking and going over sermons, God spoke. "Who do you think is going to pray for your children if you will not?" I will not soon forget that intrusion of the Almighty into my reverie.

7. Pray or else you are on your own.

In prayer we are saying, "Lord, thy will be done." In refusing to pray, we are demanding that our will be done. And that request, we might add, will be granted. The Lord goes nowhere He's unwanted.

The old hymn goes, "The arm of flesh will fail you; you dare not trust your own."

God lets us learn that lesson the hard way in the school of experience.

The flipside to "Without me you can do nothing"–the sum of all the "or elses" above–is Paul's eloquent testimony: "I can do all things through Christ who strengthens me" (Philippians 4:13).

CHAPTER EIGHT

The Biggest Problem with Prayer

This is one that almost never gets addressed. It was put to me in a note from my friend Nancy Johnson, now with the Lord in Heaven.

I need you to help me understand why we are told when we pray and believe our prayers will be answered. Then people die in spite of our pleas for health. I know it is within God's will but why ask if His will is what is going to occur anyway? I know thousands of prayers were said for (a friend who died some years back) and for my friend I saw buried today. Thousands are being said for (a friend with cancer) yet she is in a battle for her life.

We are told "you have not because you ask not." Maybe this would be a good blog topic. I can't be the only one who struggles with these thoughts.

If you only knew, Nancy.

Most of the books on prayer, and most of the many articles I've written on the subject, skirt around this question.

So, let's try to meet it head on.

Let's start by this upfront admission: **Things are not as simple as they seem at first.**

Frankly, as one who likes things simple and cut-and-dried, this is painful to admit.

The Bible actually does say things like: "Ask and it will be given to you; seek and you will find; knock and it will be opened to you. For everyone who asks receives...." (Matthew 6:7-8) And this: "Whatever you ask in my name, that I will do, that the Father may be glorified in the Son. If you ask anything in my name, I will do it" (John 14:13-14).

There are plenty more, but those two are sufficient to establish that the blanket promises are out there.

What are serious disciples of the Lord Jesus to make of such prayer promises?

1. The apostles clearly did not understand these as blank checks.

Had they interpreted these promises as "get-out-of-jail-free" cards, they would have cashed them in. At the first sign of trouble, they would have "named it and claimed it" and poof! all is well.

That is not what we see happening in the early church.

Instead, we see Jesus Himself enduring great "contradiction of sinners against himself" (Hebrews 12:3) to the point of going to the cross and submitting to death at the hand of sinners (Philippians 2:8 and I Peter 2:21ff., among other places).

We see the first generation of disciples undergoing great persecution, even to the point of death. In fact, not only does it seem that they did not "cash that card," they actually "rejoiced that they were found worthy to suffer shame for His name" (Acts 5:41) and used the suffering as a means of authenticating their witness (Acts 16:25ff).

There is no place in the Bible which indicates that the apostles interpreted Jesus' statements as blanket promises to anyone who believes and asks.

I grant you that's what those verses in the gospels seem to say. Were it left to us; I expect most of us would tweak such passages to clear up any misunderstandings.

I say this cautiously, recognizing that my words sound suspiciously like I'm criticizing the Lord. I'm not. If anything–in my mind, at least–I'm being critical of the way the gospel writers left these promises hanging. Remember what the Apostle Peter said concerning Paul's writings in Second Peter 3:15-16, that some are hard to understand.

The Holy Spirit inspired these words, yes. So, we thank Him and try our best to make the most of them. As the ancient gospel song said, "We'll understand it all by and by."

2. The most reliable way to interpret God's word has always been to compare scripture with scripture.

"No scripture is of private interpretation," said the Apostle in Second Peter 1:20. Now, that could mean no individual is to go off on a tangent by his lonesome promoting his own personal interpretation. Or, it may be saying that scripture must not be taken out of context and isolated but interpreted within the fullness of revelation. Or both. Or, even additional things.

Almost every Bible teacher I've ever known of any denomination holds that every promise of Jesus (or any other passage) should be placed in its proper setting alongside the rest of the Bible's revelations on each subject.

Scripture has much to say about which prayers God answers and which He doesn't, why some are answered, and others seem to go into God's file 13. Here are a couple:

"Your iniquities have separated you from God; and your sins have hidden His face from you, so that He will not hear" (Isaiah 59:2). Sin blocks the reception of prayer.

"The effective, fervent prayer of a righteous man avails much" (James 5:16). Prayer should be heart-felt and the prayer should be righteous.

3. The biggest element in our praying must always be faith.

"Without faith it is impossible to please God" (Hebrews 11:6).

The Lord said to the disciples, "Why did you fear; where is your faith?" (Mark 4:40)

To a distraught father, Jesus said, "If you can believe, all things are possible" (Mark 9:23).

But there is a major problem here. We can believe as strongly as it's possible to do, and sometimes the heavens seem silent. This has given rise to all sorts of abuse as unscrupulous charlatans who know more about conning people than they do Scripture browbeat their victims into believing prayers are unanswered because they do not have sufficient faith.

Some years ago, a professor at Oral Roberts University wrote a book which I found helpful. *From the Pinnacle of the Temple* by Charles Farah points out the vast gulf between doing something by faith–that is in obedience to the Word and to the leadership of the Spirit–and doing it presumptuously (God has not promised it, commanded it, or desired it, but we do it anyway).

Just because we have faith, we do not get all we ask.

The Lord who promised that "if you had faith as a grain of mustard seed, you could move mountains" (Luke 17:6) clearly does not hand out answers to prayer according to the size of one's belief.

And, as if we needed further complications, sometimes in the Word, Jesus responds to the faith of one person by blessing another. In Mark 2:5, it was the faith of the four pallet-bearers that impressed the Savior sufficiently that He forgave and then healed the paralytic. Not a word about the faith of the sick fellow is mentioned.

We always do well to believe on the Lord Jesus Christ. As someone has stated it, this means: "With all I know of me, I put my trust in all I know of Him."

4. Even if all the other elements are present, the ultimate deciding factor is the will of God.

Imagine for a moment the chaos which would follow if God gave you and me a divine formula, which, when followed, could end all disease and extend life indefinitely.

No one would ever die. No one would stay unemployed longer than a day. No child would go hungry. No heart would ever stay broken.

It would be heaven. (And Heaven itself would be empty.)

But this world is not heaven. It is a fallen world where sin and evil are at work, where the prince of darkness is on the job, and where mysteries humans cannot imagine are playing out at every moment.

Our God is in the heavens; He does whatever He pleases (Psalm 115:3).

Christian, you're going to be needing that truth in your toolbox. There will be times aplenty when the only answer we can give is: God knows what He is doing.

This is not to say God wills for that young mother to die of cancer, leaving behind those little babies.

God does not will for the infant to be run over by that truck in the mobile home parking lot or the father of three teenagers to die in his 40s.

So, why does it happen?

Underline this one, my friend, and burn it on your heart: **Not everything that happens in this world is God's will.**

My friend Nancy asked, "Why should we ask if His will is what is going to occur anyway?" Others put it this way: "Since God's will always gets done, why bother to ask?"

God's will does not always get done. If it did, then we could blame everything in this world on God.

Get straight on this, friend. This is a fallen world and sin is afoot. Satan has much to account for. And his day of reckoning is coming. (Which accounts for his anger, according to Revelation 12:12.)

It's easy to discount sin. People do it all the time. We speak of babies coming into the world as blank slates and ready for us to write on them. We speak of this as being the best of all possible worlds. We sing of how "this is My Father's world."

It is indeed His world. But we must not forget the snake in the garden. He is at work charming the gullible, fooling the blind, and conning the know-it-alls.

6. Ultimately, after we've done all we know to do, we have to end by saying, "Even so, Father, Thy will be done."

Whatever you decide, Father, let's do that.

Corrie ten Boom and countless others, including my wonderful Grandmother Bessie McKeever, noted that this life is like a weaving, the underside of which is all we see. The master weaver blends in dark and gold for a pattern seen only by His eyes. Eventually, but only when we get "on top," will we discern the pattern. Until then, we walk by faith.

We said above that the biggest element is our faith. But the truest expression of our faith is submission to the will of the Father.

In Gethsemane, Jesus wanted the Father to save mankind by any other method if one was available. But there wasn't. He prayed, *"O my Father, if it is possible, let this cup pass from me; nevertheless, not as I will, but as you will"* (Matthew 26:39).

That's where we have to leave this subject.

We are to ask Him for what we need. We are to ask in faith. We are to submit ourselves into His hands to do with as He pleases. But we are not to demand, not to be presumptuous, and not to claim what He has not promised.

Nothing about this is simple. If it were, good people would not differ.

Someone once said, "We read the Bible and interpret it away to nothing. One of these days, someone is going to come along and read it and believe it, and the world will be changed forever."

That sounds so good, I promise you it will garner a truckload of "amens" at a preachers' meeting.

But it's wrong.

God's word always has to be interpreted. It must not be lifted out of context and made to mean what was never intended.

Let the people of the Lord demand that their teachers and pastors give them the whole teaching of God and not isolated bits and pieces which they've turned into panaceas. Let the people of God grow up in their love for all the Word and their appreciation for ministers who cater not to the fancies of the shallow but will obey the One who said, "Feed my sheep" (John 21:17).

In the meantime, while we are in this world with needs galore all about us, let us be faithful in praying. And after we have prayed by faith, let us leave the results in the hands of the Lord, giving thanks for all that comes, whatever that happens to be.

CHAPTER NINE

The Simplest Prayer: "Lord, Help Me!"

My mother's Alzheimer's taught me something about prayer.

Years ago, as a young pastor visiting nursing homes, I would hear patients calling out, "Help me! Would somebody help me?" as I walked down the hall.

"What's wrong with the staff here?" I wondered. "Why aren't they helping this poor soul?"

After my wonderful mother came down with Alzheimer's or one of its relatives (senility, dementia) in the last couple of years of her life, our family tried to take care of her in her own home. Once, when I spent a long weekend there contributing what I could to her care, I came home and wrote about it.

That's what follows here....

"Help me," Mom calls out repeatedly. Even when she's feeling fine and seems to have no needs at all, she repeats this. If you ask, "What do you want, mom?" she doesn't have an answer. She seems to have been unaware she was saying that.

On one occasion, as I awakened from a brief afternoon nap, I heard mom in the next room. "Help me. Help me." I walked in and said brightly, "Mom, would you like some ice cream?" She stopped her little chant and said brightly, "Yes, I think I would." I had to laugh at the speed of that transition.

A few days later, on the way to church, I sent up a quick prayer to the Heavenly Father. "Lord, help me please." And just as clearly I heard His answer.

"What exactly are you asking me to do for you?"

I was calling for help in the way of Alzheimer patients, without thought and with no specific need in mind. The little prayer was just a mental spasm, an involuntary sense of spiritual need directed heavenward but without any sense of direction.

After he had prayed continually "Jesus, Son of David, have mercy on me," the blind beggar of Jericho was brought to stand in front of the Savior. He heard the voice of the Lord say something no one had ever asked him before: *What do you want me to do for you?* (Luke 18:41).

As a beggar, Blind Bartimaeus had lived off the cast-offs and hand-me-downs from society. He had taken scraps and the dregs and the loose change of everyone. No one had ever looked him in the eye with respect and said, "What can I do for you?" It's the question of a servant. *What can I do to help you?*

Our Lord was asking him to get specific.

Until that moment, Jericho's blind beggar had been begging for mercy. Mercy is a broad category and could cover a multitude of requests: money, a better begging place, a training program for the blind, kinder treatment from the citizens, clothes, food, healing. The Lord was simply wanting the blind beggar to identify his need and bring it to Jesus.

The Lord Jesus refuses to impose His blessing on anyone.

Scripture tells us "You have not because you ask not" (James 4:2).

In his book, "Pray Big," Will Davis Jr. talks about the power of "pinpoint praying." He writes, "God wants us to be strategic and focused about what we're asking Him to do. We need to pray for things—very specific things, gritty things, personal things, important things, kingdom things—with the pinpoint precision that Jesus modeled in the Lord's Prayer."

Will Davis has three suggestions for us.

First, he says, **keep your prayer simple.**

Davis says, "We've made prayer too complicated. My own bookshelves and hard drives are filled with guides, tools, and aids that are supposed to help me pray better. The problem is that I have to learn the program or concepts on which each of these well-meaning tools is based."

Second, **make your prayer specific.**

Davis suggests we consult the Lord's Prayer in search for anything vague or nonspecific.

"Everything Jesus spoke had focus and clarity."

And third, **keep your prayer biblical.**

Davis says, "Praying the Bible takes all the guesswork out of prayer. Right at your fingertips there is an arsenal of pinpoint prayers that you know God will answer."

The one thing that the author did not suggest–something we might have expected–is that we pray small prayers. While it's in order to ask God for the infinitesimal as well as the infinite, Will Davis Jr. urges us to "pray big."

In his book 'Built to Last,' leadership guru Jim Collins encourages readers to set what he calls BHAGs. "Big, hairy, audacious goals."

Will Davis likes that and suggests we need to start praying BHAPs.

"A big, hairy, audacious prayer is the kind of prayer that takes your breath away. It's a vision so God-sized, so humanly impossible, and yet so utterly appealing that it totally consumes you–and it drives you to your knees in prayer."

So, what kind of help do you need today? Why not tell the Lord in no uncertain terms what you need from Him?

Thou art coming to a King;

Large petitions with thee bring.

For His grace and power are such,

None can ever ask too much.

–John Newton

Note from Joe: Well, I guess we covered the bases here. Back in chapter 4, we said you should pray small. And in chapter 8, we said to pray big. Consistent, we are not! (Smile, please.) Maybe we need a chapter now saying Pray Both Ways!

CHAPTER NINE

Uh, Friend. About Your Poor Prayer

> *.... We do not know how to pray as we should.... (Romans 8:26)*

I find it liberating to know that the great Apostle Paul was dissatisfied with his prayer life. At least, that's how I read Romans 8:26. And if he could admit that "we do not know how to pray as we should," it's a lead pipe cinch that you and I don't either.

One thing almost everyone in your congregation has in common on a typical Sunday morning is a dissatisfaction with their prayer life. That is not to say that all are doing poorly, only that none of us feels we have got it down right, that we are praying with the effectiveness we'd like.

In this life, we are always going to be doing things partially. "We know in part," Scripture says. "We prophecy in part" (I Corinthians 13:9,12).

We pray poorly.

Good music, they say, is music that is written better than it can be played. The Christian life is like that: written better than any of us can hope to attain in this life. The standard of God is still the same: "Be ye perfect even as your Father in Heaven is perfect" (Matthew 5:48). We will not attain it in this life, but that's how it's written.

So with your prayer life. You and I mumble in our prayers, like a child still learning to talk. It frustrates us and disappoints us, but—do not miss this—is oddly pleasing to the Father in Heaven.

Here are seven statements about your and my poor praying....

1. Our poor praying is a fact.

We feel it often. In fact, unless you are one in a thousand, the fact that your praying is so poor has sometimes discouraged you from even trying to speak to the Father. It's so important to know that you are not the odd man out.

We are all in the same boat.

You and I have lots of company. The preacher with a half-century of church experiences still approaches the Throne of Grace like a beginner, still coming humbly almost as a newcomer. "Nothing in my hand I bring; simply to Thy cross I cling."

We must not let this upset us or discourage us from praying.   In fact....

2. Our poor praying is the norm.

Take the Olympics. Only the best in the world, the most accomplished, make it there, earning the privilege of going head to head with one another. No athlete who makes it to this point is satisfied just to achieve average in their athletic endeavors. Likewise, in our praying we want to forge ahead, to discipline ourselves to learn and grow. But, be warned: There will never come a time in this life when we will feel we have arrived in our praying.

I cringe when someone calls me a great prayer warrior, as one did just this week. I know better than that. I'm a babbler, a mumbler, a sinner with no right in myself to approach the Lord, one who comes deserving only judgment. I pray poorly. Furthermore, in this life, I seriously doubt there will come a time when that changes.

3. Our poor praying is all of faith.

Nothing we do in this life is more about faith than praying. When we pause to offer a prayer to God, we are talking to One whom we cannot see and cannot prove exists. We cannot guarantee that He hears us or that if He does, He will answer and grant our request. And yet we keep praying.

Most of our prayer requests in this life, we will never know whether they are answered or not. We will pray for the President of this country, for missionaries around the world, and for family members near and far. But we will have no way of knowing what God did in answer to our prayer.

We will pray by faith or gradually lose heart and quit. (II Corinthians 4:1 works here.)

4. Our poor praying is powerful and effective.

God does not turn away in disgust from our poor praying because we did not use the right words, take the correct posture, address Him in just the right way, or line up our doctrine in accordance with some official creed. As a loving parent thrills to hear the poor speech of the toddler, our Father in Heaven loves it when we pray.

The prayers He answers are almost always poor prayers. Had He been on a fault-finding mission, He could have failed almost every one of those prayers for a hundred reasons. But He doesn't.

One Saturday, I spent the afternoon sketching people at a block party for Hammond, Louisiana's Old Zion Hill Baptist Church. All day heavy showers had been drenching the southeastern part of the state. As I drove up, I was afraid the event would be drowned out. However, the church was high and dry. The pastor's wife told me why.

She showed me the weather radar on her phone. "I made pictures of it," she laughed. Earlier that morning, when she had seen that the weather picture indicated rain coming their way, she commented to her daughter that they might get rained out. "Mom," she said, "God parted the waters of the Red Sea. He certainly can handle this."

"Look at this," she said to me. On her iPhone, there were the various photos of the radar from earlier in the day. As the rain approached the area around Hammond-Tickfaw, the green split and left it high and dry.

We had a sobering moment. Had God done that? The pastor's daughter thinks so. Who am I to tell her He didn't? (Psalm 115:3 says He does whatever He pleases.)

"More things are wrought by prayer," said Alfred Lord Tennyson, "than this world knows of."

5. Our poor praying is no excuse.

It's a fact that we pray poorly, but that is no excuse to quit praying, to stop learning how to pray better, to stop growing, for not believing, and for not obeying.

In fact, knowing that the Living God will hear the flawed intercessions and faulty praise of imperfect children like us is liberating and encouraging.

So, don't stop praying, Christian, just because you don't feel your prayers are getting anywhere. You're not the judge. Pray on.

6. Our poor praying is God's opportunity.

"The Lord helps us in our weakness," Scripture says. "He intercedes for us with groanings too deep for words" (Romans 8:26).

You're familiar with Second Corinthians 12 where Paul learned that our weakness is God's opportunity to do something special, to show Himself mighty, to get all the praise and glory for Himself. Therefore, the apostle said, "I am well content with weaknesses, with insults, with distresses, with persecutions, with difficulties, for

Christ's sake; for when I am weak, then I am strong" (I Cor. 12:10).

For reasons He alone knows, God delights in using the poor and small, the overlooked and ordinary, the despised and the discarded. Like you and me.

7. Our poor praying is temporary.

"Now we see in a mirror dimly, but then face to face; now I know in part, but then I shall know fully, just as I also have been fully known" (First Corinthians 13:12).

The day will come when we stand in His presence and we shall be changed into His likeness. At that moment, we shall know. We shall be made perfect. "This corruption must put on incorruption; this mortal must put on immortality" (Second Corinthians 15:53).

At that moment, we will be able to pray well. We will finally know how to address the Father in the best way, using the right words, knowing His will perfectly and how to present ourselves into His presence.

Until then, we shall walk by faith. We will obey Him and offer our prayers in our faltering manner, using our poor choice of words, knowing anyone can find fault with them, doing the best we can, knowing that He is a God of mercy and kindness and loves us more than we could ever deserve.

Jesus said, "Your Father knows what things you have need of before you ask Him. Pray then like this: 'Our

Father who art in Heaven, hallowed be Thy name...."
(Matthew 6:8ff.)

CHAPTER TEN

I Prayed For My Preaching--And Got Answers I Did Not Expect.

I had been preaching for more than two decades and should have been at the top of my game. The church I served ran up to 1,500 on Sunday mornings, and the live telecast of our services covered a fair portion of several states. Most of my colleagues thought I had it made, and if invitations to speak in other churches were any sign, they thought I could preach.

But I didn't think that.

My confidence was taking a beating as some of the leaders let me know repeatedly that my pulpit work was not up to their standards. Previous pastors carried the reputation of pulpit masters, something I never claimed for myself. To make matters worse, we had numerous vacancies on staff and my sermon preparation was suffering because of a heavy load of pastoral ministry. But you do what you have to do. Most days, my goal was to keep my head above water. Every day without drowning became a good day.

That's when I got serious about praying for my preaching. Each night I walked a four-mile route through my neighborhood and talked to the Father. My petitions dealt with the usual stuff–family needs, people I was concerned about, and the church.

Gradually, one prayer began to recur in my nightly pleadings.

"Lord, make me a preacher."

Yep. That's what I was asking.

"Make me a preacher."

Praying this felt so right I never paused to analyze it. I prayed it again and again, over and over, for weeks.

I was in my fifth pastorate. I owned a couple of seminary degrees. I had read the classics on preaching and attended my share of sermon workshops. I was a veteran. But here I was in my mid-forties, crying out to heaven for help: "Lord, make me a preacher."

I knew if my preaching improved, if the congregation felt better about the sermons, everything else would benefit. I knew that the sermon is a pastor's most effective contribution to the spiritual lives of his members. To do well there would ease the pressure in other areas. So I prayed.

Then one night, God answered.

FOUR SPECIFIC REQUESTS

Without warning, in the quietness of a dark night on the city streets, God spoke within me: "What exactly do you mean by that?"

The question hit with such force that I laughed aloud and said, "What a great question. Wonder what I do mean?"

For the rest of my walk, I pondered God's probing of my too-general prayer. I knew I was not asking for public acclaim or to be on anyone's list of great preachers. I just wanted to be effective, to do well what God had called me to do.

Later that night, at home, I listed four specific requests and began to direct them toward the Father.

--I never want to stand up to preach again without a good grasp of the Scripture.

I'm tired of not being clear about the text in front of me.

--I want the message from God to have a firm grasp on me, to grip my heart.

I want to preach with genuine passion.

--I want a good rapport with the congregation.

I'm tired of that glazed overlook on the people's faces. I want to contact them, to communicate effectively.

--I want to see lives changed.

If the point of preaching is for the Word of God to make a difference in people, then it must be in order to ask the Father to grant me success in doing it.

That night, I learned something about my prayer life. For years, my prayers had been tainted by the curse of generality. It had been "bless this" and "help that" and "strengthen him" and "encourage her." One day I noticed in Luke 18:35-43 this interchange between the Lord and blind Bartimaeus, whose plaintive cries of "Jesus, have mercy on me" had reached the ears of our Lord. Over and over, the beggar of Jericho called into the air for mercy, over the shushing and objections of locals who were embarrassed by his carryings-on.

"Bring him to me," Jesus said. When Bartimaeus stood before Him, our Lord said, "What do you want me to do for you?"

We moderns are tempted to rebuke the Lord for His callousness at this point. "Lord," we would say, "anyone can see what he needs. He's been begging for mercy. He needs his sight." But the question was whether Bartimaeus knew this. He could just as easily have asked for money, for a better begging site, for assistance, for a training program for the blind, or for a hundred other things.

The Lord simply asked the man to be specific in his prayer: "What do you want?"

"Lord," he said, "I want to receive my sight."

"Then do," said the Savior. And he did.

From that point on, I prayed these four requests in my nightly walks: a good grasp of Scripture, its firm grasp on me, good rapport with my listeners, and changed lives.

Soon I was without a pulpit and without a church.

GOOD NEWS FROM EXIT INTERVIEWS

The conflict in the church I was serving escalated to the point that we brought in a mediator. He interviewed church leaders, watched videos of my preaching, and polled the congregation, then filed his report. "Joe is not a pulpit giant," he said, "but he is a pretty fair preacher." I was encouraged by that. Then he recommended I leave the church.

I agreed. I took a one-year leave of absence and I waited by the phone. A few invitations for revivals and conferences came in during the year; however, none but the tiniest churches would consider me as a potential pastor. My confidence in my preaching was at an all-time low.

Not by coincidence, the church that called me as pastor a year later was also at an all-time low. It had suffered a disastrous split. Half its thousand members had left, and the remainder was burdened with a great load of debt. Our first five years together were not easy. Gradually, however, we began to see the Lord was up to something special. One day I looked around and realized we had become a healthy church again, one that was a pure joy to serve.

That's when the other surprise appeared, one just for me. After attending a Saddleback conference on purpose-driven churches, we began sending response cards to church visitors. These notes trickled back into the church office, telling what our guests had noticed first, liked best, and appreciated least about their visit to our church. To my utter amazement, many were impressed by the preaching.

I still recall standing at my secretary's desk reading two cards that had arrived in the morning mail. Both expressed thanks for my sermons. "I am totally surprised," I mumbled.

She looked up from her work. "Pastor, everyone loves your preaching."

"I guess I didn't know it," I replied.

To be honest, I'm still not quite convinced. But I've decided that's all right. The object of my prayers was never that people would like my preaching. It wasn't even that I would like it. It was a prayer for effectiveness in doing what God called me to do.

Good music, it is said, is music that is written better than it can be played. Perhaps that's how it is with the gospel of Christ. The message is far superior to any human expression of it. A gracious Father takes the efforts of his frail servants and uses them to change lives.

Next year marks my fortieth anniversary in ministry, and I still feel inadequate about my preaching. Not only is that all right, I think it's the appropriate way to feel about a calling so far above the capacity of any of us mortals–to proclaim the riches of Christ in human tongue.

It forces me to pray for my preaching.

CHAPTER ELEVEN

Why we pray for revival and it does not come

"...you were unwilling." (Matthew 23:37)

One. We do not want revival. Not really.

Two. God does not trust us with a revival, and for good reason. He refuses to arm an enemy, to endow a rebel.

There! Those are the answers to the question.

Now, pull up a chair and let's talk about it.

It's that plain and simple: we really do not want a Heaven-sent, life-rearranging revival.

We want the results, the good part, but not the upheaval in our personal lives, priorities, and schedules which a Heaven-sent revival would cause.

We want our churches filled, the community changed, and the believers encouraged. What we do not want is to be caught up in a spiritual fervor that drives us to resign certain affiliations, stop certain activities, and devote ourselves to lengthy prayer meetings and Bible studies and ministry.

We want the harvest without the cost. We want certain aspects of the harvest, but not all.

So, our loving God will not force revival on us.

We almost wish He would. "This is for your own good," He might say, as He force-fed His good things down our church steeples and into our hearts and homes and fellowships.

But no. The Lord has chosen to set His blessings before us and to let us decide whether we are willing to receive them on His terms.

Jesus told the church at Laodicea: "I stand at your door and knock. If anyone hear my voice and open the door, I will come in and will sup with him and he with me" (Revelation 3:20).

The Lord is so eager to bestow Heaven's goodness that He brings it right up to our door. But He is so respectful of our right to decide for ourselves that He stops there, makes Himself available, and waits for us to choose.

We get to choose.

We have to choose.

"The word is nigh thee and, in thy mouth," Paul told the church at Rome. He said, "That if you confess with your mouth 'Jesus is Lord' and believe in your heart that God raised Him from the dead, you will be saved" (Romans 10:8-9).

God is not playing hard to get with us. He puts Heaven's blessings on the lowest shelf so even a child can reach them.

In fact, Jesus says becoming a child is the correct way to access Heaven. (Matthew 18:3)

Why then are we not saved? Why are we not receiving Heaven's blessings on a regular basis? Why are our churches not experiencing continual revival?

Put another way, why do we limp along under the burden of our failures and addictions and fears, while our churches go through the motion of faithfulness and see little of the fruit of righteousness?

Where is the Lord's blessings in our lives and churches?

The problem is with us, not with God.

He's available. Jesus told the leper of Mark 1, "I am willing," as He did the unthinkable and touched the untouchable and made the man whole.

God is willing for you to be saved (see Second Peter 3:9), willing to pour out Heaven's gifts upon us (see Romans 8:32), willing to give to those who ask (Matthew 7:11).

We are the snag, the bottleneck, the frog in the pipe.

Dr. John "Bud" Traylor tells of a college dorm where the water had stopped flowing through the pipes. As the plumber ran his lines, he made a discovery. A tadpole in the waterline had grown larger and larger until it filled a pipe and blocked the flow of the water. The plumber cleaned out the pipe, and the water flowed again.

The offending blockage is all our doing.

We simply do not want revival enough.

We want the fruits of revival. We would like to see lives changed, society transformed, schools safe and peaceful and joy-filled, homes reclaimed, and marriages saved.

What we do not want is to have to pay the price to get these effects.

Honestly. If the Lord were to tell your church that by praying 2 hours a night for two weeks, a Heaven-sent revival would pervade the community unlike anything ever seen, I predict that half the congregation would yawn in His face and tell the pastor to get started with his prayer program.

We want the fruits without sowing the seed or cultivating the tender growth.

That's why we do not have revival.

God refuses to arm a rebel.

Were the Lord to pour out blessings on a son or daughter living in open sin and rebellion, He would be violating His own will, endowing the rebel with resources to continue in wayward paths, and blessing the person attacking Him.

A longtime friend who had recently retired was invited to become pastor of a small church that would be "just right" for this time in his life. As he had preached there a number of times over the past months, the pastor knew of a problem within the congregation, and was assured by the deacons it would be dealt with if only he would agree to become the pastor.

Two of the leaders of that church–a deacon and a woman in the choir–were living together as husband and wife but were unmarried. Everyone knew it but no one had the courage to address it. The pastor said this couple were most outspoken in their Christianity and quick to judge others for not doing their share around the church.

After some months, the deacon chair told the pastor they would not be dealing with the matter. "I guess we're just cowards," he admitted.

That's when my friend took it upon himself to speak to the couple.

The matter quickly blew up and the woman began to attack him verbally in the community. Church members, long accustomed to letting this Jezebel rule the roost, encouraged the pastor to leave well enough alone.

So, the pastor resigned.

In informing me of his decision, he said, "As you know, you are scheduled to preach a revival for that church next month. It's up to you whether you want to go or not."

I said, "Please tell them I am withdrawing." Scripture says, "If I regard iniquity in my heart, the Lord will not hear me" (Psalm 66:18).

All of them are living in sin. The man and woman who openly flout God's laws are in sin, and the church leaders and members who tolerate it share the blame.

To try to have a revival while openly disobeying God would be to insult the Heavenly Father.

Until we are willing to "present (our) bodies a living sacrifice," to do whatever it takes to be available to the Heavenly Father, there will be no revival and we may as well stop asking.

However, if we are willing to do His will above all things, then let us ask and ask and keep on asking until Heaven arrive in force. "Pray without ceasing."

Will you join the rest of us in praying for revival? And if no one else is praying--if you are alone in this intercession--will you keep praying until God sends the revival of His choosing?

"When the Son of Man comes, will He find faith on earth?" (Luke 18:8)

CHAPTER TWELVE

How to Pray Fresh Prayers

"I will sing a new song to Thee, O God...."
(Psalm 144:9)

The message from a friend raised a question I'd not thought of: "Can you tell me how to freshen up my prayer time? My prayers all sound the same after a while. I get tired of my own words, so I know the Lord must."

Great question. How indeed do we freshen up our prayers?

Herewith my thoughts on that subject. (Remembering the opening words of this book, I speak as an expert on absolutely nothing. Consider this simply as one believer encouraging another.)

1. Freshness is overrated.

When my grandchild enters the room, I'm not listening for something new from her. She crawls into my lap, hugs my neck, and speaks the same words I have heard again and again, but which never grow old or stale: "I love you, Grandpa."

I love you, too, honey.

2. Freshness may be more for us than for the Lord.

Since He sees the heart and knows the mind before a thought is formed, it's not as if our Heavenly Father "needs" a new or better expression of our devotion. This is why, so long as our hearts are in it, prayers and scriptures we have memorized may still be effective in drawing us closer to the Heavenly Father. What the Lord seems not to care for are mindless recitations of memorized prayers.

I frequently begin my prayer period with scriptures I memorized decades ago but which continue to inspire me. "My soul doth magnify the Lord; my spirit rejoices in God my Savior" (Luke 1:46-47). "I will call upon the Lord who is greatly to be praised; So shall I be saved from my enemies. The Lord liveth; and blessed be the Rock and let the God of my salvation be exalted" (Psalm 18:3,46).

I recite the Lord's prayer, sometimes more than once if I sense my mind is wandering or not getting into the meaning of those words.

3. Nothing teaches us how to pray and to pray freshly like the Holy Scriptures.

a) We see how others prayed and are instructed by the pattern of their praise and intercessions.

I love the prayer of Elijah at Carmel: "Lord, let these people know there is a God in Israel and (while you're at it) that I am your servant!" (First Kings 18:36). As a pastor, I prayed that repeatedly when it seemed some in the congregation were laboring night and day to undermine my leadership or countermand what I was preaching. And, I'm happy to report, the Lord answered.

b) We read a passage and are inspired to "pray those same words." Praying Scripture–that is, asking the Lord to do in us what He said in that text–is always a great way to lift our intercessions out of the doldrums.

Praying the Beatitudes, we would ask that the Lord would help us to be poor in spirit that we might receive the kingdom of Heaven, that we might mourn over the sinful condition of our world in order to receive His comfort, that we might be gentle and thus inherit the earth.

Jesus taught the pathway to greatness is through serving people (Matthew 19:26-28). So, either privately in my closet or publicly in a worship service, it would be worthwhile to pray for this–for the desire to serve (not just occasionally but as a way of life), for the willingness to lay ambition and self-centeredness on His altar daily, for the love that makes servanthood authentic, and for my focus to remain on Jesus Christ and nowhere else.

c) My favorite approach is to find a verse of Scripture that "has my name on it" (that is, it seems to jump off the page, demand my attention, and insist that I camp out there for a while) and reflect on it, then pray it.

Case in point...

"How blessed is he whose help is the God of Jacob, Whose hope is in the Lord his God" (Psalm 146:5). We read that verse,

conclude there's nothing notable about it and go on. But by camping out on it, by meditating upon these words and asking the Lord to open them to us, we begin to see wonderful insights.

–He is the God of Jacob. Jacob was his original name, replaced later by Israel. Jacob was the one who lied and cheated and swindled his brother. God is the God of some mightily flawed people. And aren't we glad of that! This is encouragement. "He Himself knows our frame; He is mindful that we are but dust" (Psalm 103:14).

–God loved Jacob just where he was but loved him enough not to leave him there. So, the Lord allowed him to go through a testing/disciplining time in the household of his uncle, and later appeared to him for a time of refocusing. God took the flawed Jacob and turned him into a champion, Israel.

–This is the kind of God we serve, who is our help, our hope. Our help today (and in ages past), our hope for all the future.

–And how encouraging is that!

And so, my prayer–inspired strictly by that one verse of Scripture–might go something like this....

"Dear Lord, You have said in your holy word 'How blessed is he whose help is the God of Jacob, whose hope is in the Lord his God.' That's us, our Lord. You are our help–the One called alongside us to guide and strengthen us for the assignments you have given us.

And you are our hope—the One to whom we focus all our expectations for the future, in this life and beyond.

"We find comfort in knowing that our Heavenly Father is the One who took a weakling like Jacob, a man of many faults and flaws, and you showed great patience in leading him through the years, eventually making him a great champion of faith. Father, do that in us please.

"Be patient with our flaws; but give us victory over them. You are under no illusion about us. You knew you were getting no bargain when You redeemed us. Thank you for redeeming us, for calling us, and for your infinite patience as we have stumbled along. But make us strong. Make us champions for thee.

"Father, lift up our spirits, anchor our hopes in Thee, set our feet on the solid rock and energize us as we go forth into this day to serve Thee.

"For Jesus' sake, Amen."

The rest of Psalm 146 expounds on the theme of the Lord showing favor to the flawed and fallen.

vs 7 "He executes justice for the oppressed"

vs 8 "He opens the eyes of the blind"

vs 9 "The Lord protects the strangers; He supports the fatherless and the widow; but He thwarts the way of the wicked."

There is so much prayer material there.

d) May we do one more? Isaiah 62:6-7 gives us a prayer-insight in Scripture not mentioned anywhere else, to my knowledge. It's demonstrated again and again, but this seems to be the only place that refers to prayer as "reminding" the Lord.

"On your walls O Jerusalem, I have appointed watchmen; All day and all night they will never keep silent; You who remind the Lord, take no rest for yourselves; and give Him no rest until He establishes and makes Jerusalem a praise in the earth."

You who remind the Lord.

That's us.

When we pray, we are not telling the Lord anything He doesn't already know. "Your Father knows what you need before you ask Him" (Matthew 6:8). *He already knows, but we will remind Him.*

The Hebrew word used here is *mazkir*, from *zakar* (to remember). The word means "to cause to remember," and was the title of a court official in olden times. Sometimes called a recorder (Second Samuel 8:16; First Kings 4:3), the *mazkir* kept records of the king's business in order to remind him at critical times of promises, treaties, obligations, etc.

Now, Isaiah suggests we should think of prayer as reminding God.

This kind of prayer is demonstrated in numerous Psalms, as well as David's prayer over the materials collected to build the temple (I Chronicles 29:10-19), Solomon's prayer of dedication of that house of worship (II Chronicles 6:14-42), Jehoshaphat's prayer when Judah was invaded by a pagan coalition (II Chronicles 20:5-12), and my favorite, the early church's prayer when threatened by the religious authorities (Acts 4:23-31).

The thing to notice in these prayers is the form these people used...

–they reminded the Lord of Who He is.

–they reminded the Lord of what He had done.

–they reminded the Lord of what He had said (promised).

–and then, finally, they got to the crux of the matter. They reminded the Lord of their present situation.

–and, they reminded the Lord of what they needed, their specific request.

My favorite example of that is in Acts 4:23-30 where the church at Jerusalem prayed together when the religious authorities threatened them. It's a wonderful example.

My opinion is that the "reminding type of prayer" is not so much for bedtime or mealtime, but for important occasions when the family of God comes together.

How many other ways are there for freshening up one's prayers?

Only a thousand. Use a hymnal, borrow a Book of Common Prayer from your Episcopal friend (or do as I did and purchase one), and read books of prayers. Read books *about* praying. Go online and listen to the prayers of preachers.

Bear in mind our first two observations: 1) freshness is probably over-rated and 2) it's more for us than for the Lord.

Whatever you do, my friend, pray anyway.

Whenever you choose to pray, pray anyway.

However and for whatever reasons, pray anyway.

"The effective fervent prayer of a righteous person avails much" (James 5:16).

www.ingramcontent.com/pod-product-compliance
Lightning Source LLC
Chambersburg PA
CBHW052202110526
44591CB00012B/2046